Joie de Vivre

FRENCH PAINTINGS FROM THE NATIONAL GALLERY OF ART

Bonnard

Joie de Vivre

FRENCH PAINTINGS FROM THE NATIONAL GALLERY OF ART

Florence E. Coman, Assistant Curator,
Department of Modern Painting

Elizabeth P. Streicher, Associate Research Curator,
Department of Modern Painting

UNIVERSE

Pierre Bonnard (French, 1867–1947), A Spring
Landscape, *c. 1935, oil on canvas, .676 x 1.030, Ailsa
Mellon Bruce Collection*

Published in the United States of America in 1991
by Universe
300 Park Avenue South, New York, NY 10010

91 92 93 94 95 / 10 9 8 7 6 5 4 3 2 1

Printed in Singapore

Cover and Book Design: Christina B. Bliss

Library of Congress Cataloging-in-Publication Data

National Gallery of Art (U.S.)
 Joie de vivre: French paintings from the National Gallery of Art
 National Gallery of Art; essay by Florence E. Coman.
   p. cm.
  ISBN 0-87663-608-3
  1. Painting, French—Catalogs. 2. Painting, Modern—19th century—
France—Catalogs. 3. Painting—Washington (D.C.)—Catalogs.
 4. National Gallery of Art (U.S.)—Catalogs. I. Coman, Florence E.
II. Title.
ND547.N38 1991   91-8332
759.4'074'753—dc20   CIP

TABLE
OF
CONTENTS

Joie de Vivre

Joie de vivre is literally translated joy of life, but there is no English equivalent that adequately conveys the full meaning of the French phrase. *Joie de vivre* is an unexpected sensation, either sensory or intellectual, of pure pleasure and delight that anyone can experience. An awareness of the sheer exhilaration of living can be discovered in profound experiences but more often comes from ordinary things like seeing a rainbow after a storm, hearing a bird's song, or smelling a rose.

The thirty-two paintings selected for this book form a visual catalogue of different occasions for *joie de vivre*: a lush countryside spread out under peaceful skies, a seaside resort, a stroll in a park, a bustling city street, a festive costume ball, a calm day in a village, food on a table, flowers growing in a garden or displayed in a vase. Further, the spontaneously applied vibrant colors characteristic of impressionist painting can also be considered visual expressions of *joie de vivre*.

These paintings may appear to the viewer to be simply pleasant views of a more innocent era, a time when the world was fresh and verdant and its inhabitants healthy and handsome. The appeal of this style of painting and the charm of these subjects have made these artists universally popular. Yet the familiarity of impressionism and its apparent simplicity are deceptive, masking a variety of complex concerns, and the *joie de vivre* depicted in many impressionist paintings conceals the significant consequences of the impressionist movement. Rejecting the authority of established artistic institutions and practices, these artists asserted the fundamental freedom basic to artistic expression and transformed modern art.

Impressionism was a movement as well as a style of painting. Artists such as Claude Monet, Auguste Renoir, Camille Pissarro, Berthe Morisot, and Alfred Sisley combine both aspects of impressionism, but all who participated in the movement did not work in that style—Edgar Degas, Mary Cassatt, and Gustav Caillebotte for example—and some who did—notably Edouard Manet—did not join the movement. Yet they all contributed to what is described as the impressionist revolution.

Impressionism made its sensational debut in April 1874. A group of young artists decided to organize an exhibition, the first group exhibition independent of the official, government sanctioned Salon. Selecting a name proved difficult, so, to avoid pejorative connotations, they carefully designated themselves Artists, Painters, Sculptors, Printmakers, etc., Inc. They arranged their work in a few rented rooms on the third floor of a building on a fashionable Parisian boulevard and opened their doors a month before the Salon. Visitors were numerous, and the artists attracted attention as they had hoped, but the critical reception was mixed. Some praised the enterprise for breaking with the Salon system and were receptive to their innovations, but most established writers were harsh and derisive in their reviews.

The most notorious review was a satiric piece by Louis Leroy. He ignored the group's neutral name and, noting their unmixed pigments and broken brushwork—characteristics of unfinished sketches known as "studies" or "impressions"—as well as one work exhibited by Monet with the title *Impression, Sunrise* (Musée Marmottan, Paris), he sarcastically dubbed them impressionists, the first use of the epithet. The

Auguste Renoir, French, 1841–1919, The Dancer, *1874, oil on canvas, 1.425 x .945 (56⅛ x 37⅛), Widener Collection*

review, an invented dialogue between Leroy and an academic painter named Joseph Vincent, cleverly articulates a variety of serious objections to the artists and their enterprise. Leroy began his commentary by noting, "the rash man had come there without suspecting anything; he thought that he would see the kind of painting one sees everywhere, good and bad, rather bad than good, but not hostile to good artistic manners, devotion to form, and respect for the masters." Leroy's complaints indicate that while he considered the impressionists' paintings bad art, his principal objections lay in their deviation from what he considered artistic decency. Other journalists considered it a revolutionary, even anarchistic assault on the cultural institutions that were the foundation of the arts in France.

From the seventeenth to the nineteenth century, the government sponsored artistic expression in France by establishing and maintaining the Academy of Fine Arts. A branch of the Institute, the Academy was created to foster a national tradition in the fine arts and to pass it to succeeding generations of artists. It founded the School of Fine Arts to train young artists and the Salon, the official exhibition, to display the work of new artists and recognized masters of the Academy and to reward the most worthy participants.

The success of these well-intended institutions could be measured by the unprecedented expansion in the arts during the nineteenth century. As the number of artists competing for patronage spiraled, a jury, usually composed of members of the Academy and teachers at the School of Fine Arts, was instituted to control the quality and quantity of exhibits. Individual success came to depend on acceptance at the Salon and, consequently, on compliance with the traditional standards of the Academy.

An elaborate hierarchy existed, based on the content of a work of art. History painting, the depiction of heroic and moral lessons from ancient and modern history, religion, and literature, was most highly valued while still life and landscape painting were at the opposite end of the scale. Moreover, the style of a work of art was supposed to be appropriately ideal to correspond with the subject.

Students were taught the principles of ideal form by drawing plaster casts of antique sculpture, which they then would demonstrate in drawn studies of live models prior to instruction in multi-figure compositions and working with oil paints. The finish of a work—a smooth, polished surface created by careful gradation and blending of tones—was a prized quality. Artists prepared rough sketches in oils only as preliminary studies for finished works of art.

The 1874 impressionist exhibition was the culmination of a long struggle against Academic tradition. In the 1860s and early 1870s Salon juries grudgingly accepted a few works by the young artists, hung them poorly, or more usually rejected them. Manet, hopeful of eventual official success, persisted in submitting to the Salon, but his cohorts did not. Frustrated by reactionary juries, Monet, Renoir, Degas, Pissarro, Cézanne, Morisot, and others decided to appeal directly to the public by exhibiting as a separate group. They could show more than the two works permitted by the Salon, and conditions for viewing the works, allowing ample light and space between paintings, were preferable to the densely hung, ill-lit upper tiers to which they usually were relegated at the Salon. To mollify the public and critical reaction they invited the participation of several older, accepted artists, painters who had directly influenced the formation of impressionism such as Corot and Boudin.

In Leroy's review of the first impressionist exhibition the academician Vincent, studying a landscape, lamented, "Oh, Corot, Corot, what crimes are committed in your name!" Jean-Baptiste-Camille Corot, an established landscape painter, medalist at the Salon, and member of the Legion of Honor, declined the invitation to join the impressionists, but his influence was clearly visible in many of the works exhibited there. One of the most prolific artists of the nineteenth century, Corot practiced a relatively traditional method of working throughout his career. He would begin with the general areas of a scene, then proceed to lay in the lighter and darker masses before describing individual features of the terrain, an approach that he recommended to his pupils and followers, among them Pissarro, Morisot, Renoir, and Sisley.

Corot painted outdoors, and while his early oil sketches were preliminary studies for larger paintings to be finished in the studio, the artist gradually began to treat these studies as independent, exhibitable works. His individual and responsive handling of traditional forms and the acute, conscientious freshness of his observation that were engendered by his method of working, are evident in both *River Scene with Bridge* (Plate 1), an early oil study completed in one sitting, and in *Ville d'Avray* (Plate 2), a composed landscape painted toward the end of Corot's life.

Gustave Courbet was another artist whose work shaped the foundations of impressionism. Courbet was a realist who painted events and scenery taken primarily from his native Ornans, a village in the remote Franche-Comté region, on the grand scale reserved for history paintings. Life-size depictions of villagers and their activities such as *The Stone-Breakers* (destroyed; formerly Gemäldegalerie neue Meister, Dresden) and *Burial at Ornans* (Musée d'Orsay, Paris), considered ugly for endowing "crude" peasants with dignity and grandeur, challenged traditional ideas about art.

Courbet compounded that affront to accepted practice in 1855, the year a World's Fair was held in Paris. The selection committee for the art section, charged with assembling the greatest works of contemporary French art, rejected two of his thirteen submissions. Infuriated, Courbet withdrew. Adjacent to the Fairgrounds and concurrent with the Fair, he

Paul Cézanne, French, 1839–1906, The Artist's Father, *1866, oil on canvas, 1.985 x 1.193 (78⅛ x 47), Collection of Mr. and Mrs. Paul Mellon*

erected his own building, the Pavilion of Realism, and presented a one-man show of forty of his paintings. Realist author Champfleury described Courbet's action in a letter to a friend: "It is an incredibly audacious act; it is a subversion of all institutions associated with the jury; it is a direct appeal to the public, it is liberty." In a brochure titled *Realism,* which he distributed at his exhibition, Courbet wrote, "To be in a position to translate the customs, the ideas, the appearance of my epoch, according to my own estimation; to be not only a painter, but a man as well; in short, to create living art—this is my goal."

Courbet's assertion of the absolute necessity to depict the actuality of contemporary life rather than an idealized past echoed the words of poet and critic Charles Baudelaire, who in an 1846 review of the Salon called upon artists to depict "the Heroism of Modern Life." More than Courbet, Edouard Manet embodied the urbane modernity of Parisian experience that Baudelaire evoked. Drawing on his background in a cultured and well-to-do family he depicted his peers in *Concert at the Tuileries* (National Gallery, London). In the 1860s Manet's studio was located in an old, working class district then being torn down to make way for the modernization of Paris directed by Baron Haussmann under the mandate of Emperor Napoleon III. The people thereby displaced are the subject of *The Old Musician* (Figure 3). An ordinary gathering like the *Concert* and painted in the same year, 1862,

The Old Musician presents a loose assembly of individuals connected only by indigence and homelessness that Manet might have observed near his studio: a street musician flanked by a gypsy girl and infant, an acrobat, an urchin, a drunkard, and a ragpicker. Deliberately ambiguous, Manet neither adopts any obvious moral stance nor even conveys any information about these people beyond their appearance. Characteristic of Manet's work from early paintings like *The Old Musician* to impressionist works like *Ball at the Opera* (Plate 10) and Manet's last masterpiece, *The Bar at the Folies-Bergère* (Home House Trustees, Courtauld Institute Galleries, London) of 1882, this dispassionate detachment is a distinctly modern attitude.

Another element of Manet's work that the future impressionists admired was his style. Manet discovered that he could preserve the immediacy and directness of preliminary oil studies by placing pigments side by side as in a sketch rather than smoothly blending tones as prescribed by the Academy. This practice created sharper contrasts and crisper effects than possible with the Academic method, as evident in the abrupt transitions between lighted and shadowed areas in *The Old Musician.* Monet and Renoir emulated Manet's technique as they forged the style known as impressionism.

Other events also shaped the development of impressionism. In 1863, rejections by the Salon jury were so numerous that the emperor was forced to institute a Salon des

Refusés. Manet's *Olympia* (Musée d'Orsay, Paris) and *The White Girl* by the American painter James McNeill Whistler (National Gallery of Art, Washington) scandalized visitors, but Pissarro and Cézanne had also been rejected and showed their work there. In 1867, on the occasion of another World's Fair, the jury again rejected Monet, Renoir, Pissarro, Sisley, and Cézanne. Cézanne was one of many who petitioned the Emperor for a repetition of the 1863 Refusés, a request denied by the government. Courbet repeated his experiment of 1855 by exhibiting in a privately funded pavilion, and Manet followed his example.

Balked by continuing official intractability, Frédéric Bazille, a close friend and associate of Monet, Renoir, and Sisley, wrote his parents about "the plan of a group of young people to have their separate exhibition." Insufficient funds forced them to abandon the project and, in Bazille's words, they "will have to re-enter the bosom of the administration whose milk we have not sucked and who disowns us." The jury was severe again in 1869, rejecting Monet, Cézanne, and Sisley. Bazille wrote his parents about the idea of holding an independent, non-juried exhibition, commenting that, "it is really too ridiculous for a considerably intelligent person to expose himself to administrative caprice, especially if medals and prizes hold absolutely no interest."

Bazille died in 1870 during the Franco-Prussian War, but the idea outlined in his 1869 letter was revived in late 1873, and the following spring the first impressionist exhibition opened. Manet, who did seek official recognition, declined to join the impressionists. He submitted three paintings and a watercolor to the jury in 1874, among them *Ball at the Opera* (Plate 10), which was rejected, and *Gare Saint-Lazare* (National Gallery of Art, Washington), which gained admission. In spite of Manet's refusal to participate, critics identified him as the leader of the group rather than Monet, Renoir, Pissarro, Sisley, and Degas, who were the principal organizers. United in their opposition to the authority of the Academy, those artists also shared a preference for distinctively modern subjects and presentation.

While Louis Leroy expressed a negative perspective, other writers were more receptive. Of Pisaarro's *Orchard in Bloom* (Plate 7) one writer noted that "vulgarities of taste do not alter his beautiful qualities of execution." Pissarro's landscape, a rural gardening scene, appeared vulgar to that writer because the artist avoided sentimentality and anecdote. Rather, the diminutive peasants are intrinsic accessories to the seasonal rhythms of the land, a theme Pissarro frequently explored. Impressionists like Pissarro embraced and depicted contemporary life in all its aspects, smoke-spewing factories and trains and farm and factory laborers as well as broad boulevards, fashionably clad women, and coastal resorts.

Another work that received favorable notice was Renoir's *Dancer* (Figure 1). Leroy wrote that Renoir had, "a certain understanding of color," but that Renoir's execution, particularly in the legs, was poor. In contrast a sympathetic critic wrote that the painting was:

> . . . an original conception, a kind of fairy molded in earthly forms. Nothing is more alive than her bright and tender, rosy skin. On this the heap of gauze that makes up her dress somehow delightfully blends with her luminous and tender tones. This is Realism of the great school, the one that does not feel forced to trivialize nature to interpret it.

Renoir's feathery paint handling and sensitive use of color corresponded well with his favored subjects, women and children, in single figure compositions such as the *Dancer* and in portraits. *Pont Neuf, Paris* (Plate 20) and *Madame Monet and Her Son* (Plate 21) are painted with the energy and freshness of vision indicative of Renoir's direct observation and transcription of the scene before him.

Monet, Pissarro, Sisley, and Renoir developed impressionism as a way to capture the appearance of people interacting outdoors under natural conditions. *Bazille and Camille* (Plate 15) is a preparatory study for two figures in the *Déjeuner sur l'herbe* (Musée d'Orsay, Paris) of 1865–1866, Monet's earliest attempt to make a life-size, multi-figure composition on the scale of a history painting that would depict contemporaries enjoying an ordinary outdoor activity, in this instance a picnic. For Monet, Pissarro and Sisley, the impressionist style that evolved was best suited to landscape painting, as mature works like *The Artist's Garden at Vétheuil* (Plate 17) by Monet demonstrate. Alfred Sisley, who studied with Renoir and Monet in the studio of the academic master Gleyre, was particularly responsive to variations in light and atmospheric conditions. The delicate color effects and supple brushwork in *Boulevard Héloïse, Argenteuil* (Plate 13) are hallmarks of his finest compositions.

Like Sisley, Berthe Morisot ia noted for nuanced color harmonies and sprightly paint application, as in *The Harbor at Lorient* (Plate 19). Born to a progressive upper middle class family, Morisot studied with Corot and modeled for and worked with Edouard Manet and married his brother in December of 1874. Invited to join the impressionist group, she disregarded Manet's advice and participated in the 1874 exhibition, extending financial support as well as exhibiting a selection of works including the 1869 *Harbor at Lorient*.

Edgar Degas, the principal exponent of an alternate form of impressionism, did not adopt the impressionist technique of applying unmixed pigments in broken brushwork, nor did he abandon the traditional attitudes toward finish when he joined the impressionist movement. Rather, his is an art of refinement and finesse which originated in his admiration of Jean-Auguste-Dominique Ingres, a painter and draftsman

whose portraits and history paintings are masterpieces of Academic precision and subtlety. Degas is usually identified with a few carefully chosen themes—dancers, horses, women bathing, cafés, laundresses—which the artist frequently revised, repeated, and reworked. Arbitrary framing of the edges of his compositions and the selection of unusual vantage points, characteristics which typify Degas' work, were derived from his study of the new art of photography and recently imported Japanese prints.

Usually considered a postimpressionist, Paul Cézanne was also an impressionist and showed with the group in 1874 and again in 1877 at the third group exhibition. Of all the exhibitors, his work was most vilified by critics in 1874. Only his childhood friend, author Emile Zola, mentioned him sympathetically, referring to Cézanne's "originality" and adding that he, "unquestionably has the temperament of a great painter." Cézanne's tempestuous personality was most evident in the brooding passion of paintings from the 1860s. Exaggeratedly thick slabs of pigment applied energetically create a rugged, almost sculpted surface in *The Artist's Father* (Figure 2), 1866, and convey a clear sense of the artist's uneasy relationship with the elder Cézanne. Working with Pissarro in the early 1870s, Cézanne adopted a lighter palette, enabling him to transform the emotive energy of earlier subjects into a profoundly scrupulous visual examination of such undramatic motifs as the scenery of his native Aix, bathers, portraits, and still lifes.

In spite of generally negative public reaction to their 1874 exhibition and the financially devastating outcome of an auction of paintings by Renoir, Morisot, Monet, and Sisley in 1875, the group persisted, holding seven further exhibitions

before finally disbanding in 1886. During those twelve years, impressionism evolved continuously. Individual artists developed in different directions, and only one artist, Pissarro, participated in all eight group manifestations. The transformation of the movement may also be traced through the changes that occurred from exhibition to exhibition as original impressionists resigned and new members were enlisted.

Gustave Caillebotte was the first significant addition to the group, making his debut in 1876 at the second exhibition. Inherited wealth enabled him to support the movement financially as well as artistically. Purchasing paintings by such less fortunate colleagues as Monet, Renoir, and Sisley, Caillebotte acquired a collection of impressionist masterpieces. Lively public debate erupted after his untimely death in 1894 concerning whether his collection, left to the French national museum in his will, should be accepted. Until recently Caillebotte's importance as a patron has tended to obscure his accomplishment as an artist. Now his work is recognized and appreciated, particularly for his bold perspectives and arbitrary compositions.

The second and third group exhibitions, held in 1876 and 1877, clearly affirmed the goals of the first. They included fewer participants while the number of exhibited works increased, giving a more concentrated display of the essential character of the movement. In general, critics sympathized with their repudiation of the Salon system. In 1876 Emile Zola observed that, "a revolutionary ferment is revealed which will little by little win over the Academy of Fine Arts itself, and in twenty years will transform the Salon." The artists continued to antagonize many reviewers, particularly those attached to more widely circulated publications. The most vicious began, "five or six lunatics—among them a woman—a group of unfortunate creatures stricken with the mania of ambition . . . to exhibit their works," and dismissed them because, "they take up canvas, paint, and brush, throw on a few tones haphazardly and sign the whole thing . . . ., a frightening spectacle of human vanity gone astray to the point of madness." Yet a respectable number gave positive comments about the artists and did not disparage them for deviating from accepted ideas about finish, technique, and content. They praised "very real talent" evident in some "excellent morsels of painting," recognizing that the sketchy quality of impressionist paintings was a deliberate aesthetic decision rather than evidence of sheer laziness or incompetence, as traditionalists complained.

The exhibitions mounted by the impressionists were, in part, a strategy designed to reach potential patrons usually denied them by reactionary Salon juries, but they attracted few new supporters. Moreover the French economy had weakened in 1873 and suffered a depression in 1878, and the dealer that many artists relied on for backing, Paul Durand-Ruel, could not continue to subsidize them as he had before the middle of the decade. Lured by the prospect of lucrative commissions, Renoir and Sisley defected to the Salon in 1878, and did not contribute to the impressionist exhibition the next year. The jury rejected Sisley in 1879, but Renoir's success at the Salon encouraged Monet to follow him in 1880. The group had begun to disintegrate. Even as Monet, Renoir, and Sisley distanced themselves from the impressionist enterprise, two rival factions developed, one a contingent of naturalists and landscape painters led by Pissarro and Caillebotte and the other a group of more traditional independents and realists led by Degas.

Although usually contemptuous of women artists, Degas invited Mary Cassatt to join the group in 1877. When she first appeared with them at the fourth exhibition in 1879, critics recognized her affinity to Degas. One wrote, "Degas has a student . . . whose portraits or studies of society women are worthy of serious attention," and another commented that Cassatt, "like Degas (perhaps she is his student), seeks movement, light, and design in the most modern sense." She was not Degas' pupil, but his influence on her is manifestly apparent in the crisp linear construction of the depictions of wealthy, middle class women and children for which she is known. Cassatt is also remembered for her role in introducing the impressionists to American collectors. With Cassatt's advice, her friend Louisine W. Havemeyer amassed one of the earliest and finest collections of impressionist paintings in this country, including Manet's *Ball at the Opera* (Plate 10) and exceptional works by Degas and Cézanne.

Following the example of Corot, who had earlier counselled him, Pissarro became a mentor to many young painters. Cézanne, who worked with Pissarro in 1871–1872 and

again in 1877, always acknowledged his debt to the artist he called "humble and colossal." In the last year of his own life, 1906, Cézanne paid tribute to Pissarro by labeling himself "pupil of Pissarro" in an exhibition catalogue. Paul Gauguin was another of Pissarro's disciples, and as with Cézanne, impressionism was critical to Gauguin's development. Pissarro recruited Gauguin to the group for the 1880 exhibition, and Gauguin showed in all further exhibitions.

Degas, too, actively sought new members, and his faction dominated the 1880 exhibition. Fearing a repetition as preparations were underway for the 1881 exhibition, Caillebotte wrote to Pissarro to complain that Degas, "claims that we must stick together and be able to count on each other . . . ; and whom does he bring us? Lepic, Legros, Maureau. . . . What a fighting squadron in the great cause of realism!" Caillebotte's reservations notwithstanding, Degas and his associates dominated in 1881. Instead of a painting, the most discussed work at the sixth exhibition was a sculpture, *Little Dancer Fourteen Years Old* by Degas (National Gallery of Art, Washington, Promised Gift of Mr. and Mrs. Paul Mellon, in Honor of the Fiftieth Anniversary of the National Gallery of Art). Contemporary audiences were accustomed to idealized statues in white marble or bronze; the *Little Dancer,* a statue of an awkward teenage girl made of flesh-tinted wax and wearing a hair wig tied with a ribbon and ballet dress and slippers, broke all the conventions by intentionally blurring the barriers between art and reality.

The next year Pissarro, Caillebotte, and dealer Durand-Ruel persuaded Monet, Renoir, and Sisley to return for what was to be a purely impressionist exhibition. Monet and Renoir, concerned with the quality of the exhibition, were hesitant, and Monet even wrote Durand-Ruel, "At the point where we are now an exhibition must be extremely well done or not take place at all, and it is totally necessary that we be just among ourselves, that no stain be allowed to compromise our success." Both ultimately recognized that participation was inevitable because Durand-Ruel, a prime supporter of the exhibition, could show any of the paintings that he had purchased from them, and the best recent work by all the artists was represented.

The exhibition, a critical success, paradoxically marks both the height and the passing of the impressionist era. By 1882 not only the movement but also the impressionist style was in transition. New concerns had arisen and, in contrast to their concerted development of impressionism in the late 1860s and early 1870s, the former comrades worked separately and evolved in different directions.

The line Pissarro followed carried him into the orbit of Georges Seurat, who had formulated a new technique, called divisionism or neoimpressionism, as a more scientifically accurate form of impressionism. Seurat's massive painting *Sunday Afternoon on the Island of La Grande-Jatte* (The Art

Paul Gauguin, French, 1848–1903, Self-Portrait, *1889, oil on wood, .792 x .513 (31¼ x 20¼), Chester Dale Collection*

Institute of Chicago) dominated the 1886 impressionist exhibition and propelled him to the forefront of the avant-garde. Although Seurat admired some effects in impressionist works he considered that style too spontaneous and haphazard. Preceded by numerous small preparatory sketches like *Study for "La Grande Jatte"* (Plate 28), the finished painting displayed the objective system of applying small touches of unmixed pigments according to principles of simultaneous contrast and optical mixture that Seurat developed on the basis of recent scientific discoveries about the visual properties of light and color. Pissarro, dissatisfied by the increasingly labored appearance of his paintings created by the dense webs of brushstrokes and open to new ideas, adopted this style after its 1884 introduction. Works that Pissarro included in the 1886 show were painted in the new style and, despite opposition, he persuaded others in the impressionist group to admit Seurat and his followers.

The 1886 exhibition was the eighth and last group exhibition. After abstaining in 1882, Degas and Cassatt reappeared then. Morisot and Gauguin also exhibited, while Monet, Renoir, Sisley, and Caillebotte did not. And Manet, who had finally forced the administration to concede him official honors and who had received the Legion of Honor in 1881, died in 1883, never having taken part in the exhibitions of the group whose existence he had inspired. The group disbanded after the 1886 exhibition.

The naturalist and realist impulses that were a driving force of impressionism had been supplanted by sources of inspiration that largely were symbolic and non-naturalistic, and impressionist exhibitions had already been replaced as the preeminent forum for avant-garde art by a body called the Society of Independents, whose first exhibition was held in 1884. The successor to impressionism is usually called postimpressionism. Postimpressionism does not define a style or movement as impressionism does. Rather, it is simply a term coined in 1910 to identify a variety of styles that developed out of impressionism, and is usually applied to four principal artists: Cézanne, Seurat, van Gogh, and Gauguin.

Three of the four postimpressionists had been impressionists. Cézanne became a virtual recluse after the third impressionist exhibition and, except for one anomalous and largely unnoticed showing at the Salon in 1882, did not exhibit again for twenty years. Late in life, when his fame was assured and his advice sought by younger artists, Cézanne made his famous assertion that he wanted to make of impressionism "something solid and durable like the art of museums." Working in isolation, he developed a patient, meditative style based on a system of painted notations that describe the underlying contours of a motif rather than its transitory surface appearance.

Seurat, the youngest of the four postimpressionists, was the first to explore deliberately the abstract qualities of the formal elements of painting. In works painted after 1886, for instance *Seascape at Port-en-Bessin* (Plate 29), the artist used light, color, and line—independent of subject—to convey a mood, in this instance elegiac. Seurat's development of the decorative and expressive potential of art ended with his sudden death in 1891. Many other artists, among them Pissarro, had adopted Seurat's neoimpressionist technique. Seurat became secretive to prevent others from borrowing his theory about expression. Symbolism was prevalent in contemporary French culture, however, and both van Gogh and Gauguin independently pursued similar goals, although in distinctively different ways.

Vincent van Gogh and his younger brother Theo came from a family of protestant ministers and art dealers in the Netherlands. Theo, who ran a branch office of one of Durand-Ruel's rivals, Boussod and Valadon, dealt primarily in works by academic masters but was able to create a modest impressionist section. Drawn to Paris in early 1886 by Theo's descriptions of impressionist art, Vincent became active in the most innovative circles of the avant-garde. He absorbed elements of impressionism and neoimpressionism and his palette became lighter and brushwork freer before ill health prompted van Gogh's departure to the southern town of Arles in the winter of 1888.

In the belief that working and living together would produce a fruitful exchange of ideas, van Gogh invited Gauguin, whom he had met late in 1886 in Paris, to join him in Arles. The collaboration of the two tempestuous personalities ended abruptly in a bitter fight. The precise nature of the episode is uncertain, but the result is famous: van Gogh mutilated his ear. He committed himself to a sanitarium at Saint-Rémy in 1889 after a severe breakdown; declared cured, he returned to Theo in Paris briefly in 1890, then moved to Auvers, where he committed suicide in July. The romantic myth of van Gogh's life is peripheral to his accomplishment, however, and the letters he wrote to family and a few friends during the concentrated period of his artistic maturity, from 1888 to 1890, are witnesses of the intention and determination, not madness or illness, that inform his art.

Emphatic, rhythmic brushwork and intense color and light in van Gogh's paintings create visual parallels for the artist's emotions, an aspect of van Gogh's work recognized by author Albert Aurier in the first and only article published about van Gogh during his lifetime. Aurier wrote that van Gogh was, "not only a great painter, enthusiast of his art, of his palette, and of nature, he is also a dreamer, a fanatical believer, a devourer of beautiful utopias, living on ideas and dreams." Elsewhere in the article, Aurier characterized van

Gogh's work as, "excess, excess in strength, excess in nervousness, in violence of expression. In his categorical affirmation of the character of things, in his frequently headstrong simplification of forms, in his insolence in depicting the sun face to face, in the vehement ardor of his drawing and of his color, and even in the slightest particulars of his technique, he reveals himself a powerful being, a male, a bold man, often brutal and sometimes ingenuously delicate."

In the letter written to thank Aurier for the article and to correct what van Gogh considered misapprehensions, Vincent discussed the artist with whom he is now so closely associated: "I also owe a great deal to Paul Gauguin, with whom I worked for several months in Arles and whom, besides, I already knew in Paris. Gauguin, this strange artist . . ., this friend who likes to make you feel that a good picture should be the equivalent of a good deed, not that he says this, yet it is difficult to associate with him without perceiving a certain moral responsibility."

After about 1886 Gauguin was no longer an impressionist. Reliance on the imaginative and evocative rather than concrete depiction of reality led Gauguin to theorize that, independent of the object depicted, the formal elements of a work of art, color and shape, could express meaning. Trying to explain the way this principal operates Gauguin wrote of "the musical role" of color, adding that, "color, which is vibration just as music is, is able to attain what is most universal yet at the same time most elusive in nature: its inner force." An 1889 *Self-Portrait* (Figure 4) is one of the most radical expressions of this theory. With head and hand floating on flat areas of lurid red above and ethereal yellow below, the artist suggested the demonic and angelic duality of his nature. Further, the apples and the snake he holds can be associated both with sexual temptation and with comprehensive knowledge and wisdom. Gauguin's almost caricatured depiction of his features imparts an ironic inflection to the information he presents in this image of the artist as heroic demigod.

Distrusting the sophistication of Paris, Gauguin sought nature and civilization unspoiled by modern life. Before he left for Tahiti, he worked in an artists' colony in remote northwest France. There, in 1888, the young Paul Serusier sought his advice. Gauguin went outdoors to paint with him. According to the famous anecdote, Gauguin asked, "How do you see those trees?" "Yellow," Serusier replied. "Well then," responded Gauguin, "make them your most beautiful yellow." He continued, "How do you see the earth?" "Red," said the younger man. "Use your best red," he was told. When Serusier returned to Paris he described the incident to several associates and showed them the painting. They formed a mystic cult around it, calling the painting *The Talisman* (Musée d'Orsay, Paris) and themselves the nabi, a Hebrew word for prophet.

In 1890 Maurice Denis, another nabi, enunciated the group's belief that the physical attributes of a painting, pigments arranged on a flat surface, must be recognized, and all representation was regarded of necessity as artificial. Toward the end of his manifesto Denis wrote, "Universal triumph of the imagination of aesthetes over the efforts of foolish imitation, triumph of the emotion of the beautiful over the naturalist lie. . . ." Pierre Bonnard and Edouard Vuillard were two other members of the nabi circle. Subscribing to the views articulated by Denis, works by the two friends are similar. Both preferred small-scale, intimate scenes which they developed using intricate, asymmetric surface patterns and a restricted range of color.

Decades of opposition to authority in nineteenth-century French art continually redefined the relationships between an artist and his creation and between the creator and the public, but the harsh conditions those artists endured are no longer a necessary prelude to innovation. The paintings on the following pages have been chosen both to express the *joie de vivre* that was an intrinsic aspect of their modernity, and to share it with the reader through the contemplation of their beauty. Enjoy!

Florence E. Coman
June 1991

Note to the reader:

Joie de Vivre is a brief introduction. Many books now available give a more comprehensive view of impressionism and postimpressionism and the artists who shaped their development. Chief among them are two pioneering books by John Rewald, *The History of Impressionism* (4th, rev. ed., New York, 1973) and *Post-Impressionism: from van Gogh to Gauguin* (3rd ed., New York, 1982). *The New Painting: Impressionism 1874–1886* by Charles S. Moffett (exhibition catalogue, The Fine Arts Museum of San Francisco, 1986), is an important source of information specific to impressionism and contemporary reaction, and *Impressionism and Post-Impressionism 1874–1904: Sources and Documents* (New Jersey, 1966) by Linda Nochlin is a compilation of contemporary documents related to the artists and movements. All quotations cited in the text were taken from those volumes.

JEAN-BAPTISTE-CAMILLE
Corot

FRENCH, 1796–1875

RIVER SCENE WITH BRIDGE
1834
Oil on canvas, 25 x 33.8 cm.
Ailsa Mellon Bruce Collection

One of the most notable immediate prede-
cessors of the impressionists, Corot was
trained in the classical methods of landscape
painting. When he painted this spontaneous
oil sketch in 1834, Corot had already success-
fully exhibited at the Salon. He decided he
needed further study, however, and returned
to Italy, where he had first matured as a
painter. *River Scene with Bridge* is a product
of that voyage, though the site depicted is
unidentified. Corot laid in a thin initial layer
of paint to block out the broader masses of
his composition, then superimposed a few
finer strokes to define the simple scene. The
result is a work unified by an overall blond
tonality. Throughout his career he proceeded
in this manner, painting preliminary sketches
outdoors for later elaboration into finished
works in his studio, a practice Corot recommended to both Berthe Morisot and Camille
Pissarro.

2

JEAN-BAPTISTE-CAMILLE
Corot

FRENCH, 1796–1875

VILLE D'AVRAY
c. 1867/1870
Oil on canvas, 49.2 x 65.3 cm.
Gift of Count Cecil Pecci-Blunt

Ville d'Avray was a small town about ten miles southwest of Paris, where Corot's father bought a country house in 1817. The artist visited and painted there frequently.

Corot was trained in the classical landscape tradition of Poussin and Claude. Early in his career he also executed spontaneous *plein-air* sketches, such as *River Scene with a Bridge* (see Plate 1), and painted in Fontainebleau alongside Millet, Rousseau, and the other Barbizon artists. From the 1850s on, Corot devoted most of his energies to figure pieces and to lyrical landscapes like *Ville d'Avray.* These latter canvases were well received at the Salon and brought him great commercial success.

Ville d'Avray is characteristic of Corot's late landscapes, in which he often combined real and imagined elements. Here, the pond and houses identify a specific site. However, the poetic mood, the silver, blue, and green tonalities, and the feathery brushstrokes of the foliage and vegetation are Corot's inventions and recur in many of his paintings of this period.

3

GUSTAVE
Courbet

FRENCH, 1819–1877

LANDSCAPE NEAR THE BANKS
OF THE INDRE
1856
Oil on canvas, 60.8 x 73.3 cm.
Gift of the W. Averell Harriman Foundation in
memory of Marie N. Harriman

When Courbet painted this *Landscape near the Banks of the Indre* in the mid-1850s, he had already achieved success at the Salon, and had provoked heated controversies—and inspired caricaturists—with monumental genre paintings such as *Funeral at Ornans, Young Ladies of the Village, Bathers,* and *The Studio.* From the very beginning of his career, however, he also executed more modest landscapes and portraits. Courbet painted this view of the valley of the Indre river during a visit with his friend Clément Laurier, a wealthy lawyer who entertained poets and artists at his home, the château de l'Epineau.

This landscape is traditionally composed, with a framing tree in the foreground on the left, a meandering stream leading our eye back into the middleground, and a stand of trees continuing that line into the distance. In contrast, in later works such as *Calm Sea* (see Plate 4), Courbet employed horizontal bands of beach, water and sky, and atmospheric perspective to suggest spatial recession.

4

GUSTAVE
Courbet

FRENCH, 1819–1877

CALM SEA
1866
Oil on canvas, 54.3 x 64.1 cm.
Collection of Mr. and Mrs. Paul Mellon

Like Boudin (see Plates 5 and 6), Courbet visited and painted in fashionable locales on the Normandy coast but achieved a very different result. *Calm Sea* was painted at Deauville, situated a short distance from Trouville and then its chief rival for tourist trade. In *Calm Sea* Courbet, unlike Boudin, ignored the town and its residents, permanent as well as temporary. Instead, he concentrated on the elemental purity and beauty of nature, focusing on the rectangular expanses of sky and sea. Deceptive in its simplicity, *Calm Sea* anticipates the twentieth-century taste for spare, boldly geometric compositions and experiments confidently with modernist tendencies that are more often associated with the artists of the next generation.

5

EUGÈNE
Boudin

FRENCH, 1824–1898

JETTY AND WHARF AT TROUVILLE
1863
Oil on wood, 34.6 x 57.8 cm.
Collection of Mr. and Mrs. Paul Mellon

By the early 1860s, Trouville had become
one of the most fashionable of resorts on
the northern coast of France. At the same
time, Eugène Boudin was persuaded to go to
Trouville to paint those wealthy visitors and
their recreations. Leisurely, well-clad visitors
people his paintings, sitting or strolling by
the beach, enjoying such amusements as the
casino, concerts, and the bathing huts, as
well as watching boats and ships plying the
English Channel. Here, an elegant throng
crowds the jetty, waiting for the steam ferry
as nearby strollers watch, while one pair
turns away to see a pleasure boat sail briskly
out toward open water.

6

EUGÈNE
Boudin

FRENCH, 1824–1898

FIGURES ON THE BEACH
c. 1867/1870
Oil on canvas, 38.4 x 61.3 cm.
Collection of Mr. and Mrs. Paul Mellon

As in *Jetty and Wharf at Trouville* (see Plate 5), Boudin depicts a group of stylish promenaders at a coastal resort in *Figures on the Beach.* The fresh color and sprightly brushwork evident here, similar to the emergent impressionist style, are hallmarks of Boudin's habitual working outdoors. In fact, Boudin made an important contribution to the development of impressionism: he encouraged Monet to paint outdoors with him in order to capture color and form as they exist in nature, a significant aspect of the younger man's artistic formation.

7

CAMILLE
Pissarro

FRENCH, 1830–1903

ORCHARD IN BLOOM,
LOUVECIENNES
1872
Oil on linen, 45.1 x 54.9 cm.
Ailsa Mellon Bruce Collection

When Pissarro returned to Louveciennes after the Franco-Prussian War and Commune, he found that his home had been occupied and many of his early paintings had been destroyed by enemy troops. Like the French nation, he began to rebuild. The healthy blossoms and freshly-turned earth in *Orchard in Bloom, Louveciennes,* painted the next spring, are a hopeful expression of the promise of renewal.

Pissarro had met Paul Durand-Ruel in 1871 in London, but the dealer did not begin to buy from him until March of the following year; this painting, acquired in mid-July, was one of Durand-Ruel's earliest impressionist purchases. No doubt the dealer responded to the painting's affinities to Barbizon landscape, since the firm of Durand-Ruel had specialized in works by the Barbizon masters. Pissarro had described himself as Corot's pupil in the catalogue to the Salon of 1864, and as late as 1872, Pissarro's broad method of composing—vistas dotted with small figures of peasants—still continued to evoke works by the older artist.

At Pissarro's request, Durand-Ruel lent *Orchard in Bloom, Louveciennes* to the first impressionist group show in 1874, and, of the five paintings Pissarro selected for exhibition on this special occasion, it was the first listed in the catalogue. Of course, critical reception of Pissarro and his colleagues was generally scornful then, but a few sympathetic journalists did mention the painting specifically. Castagnary's review typifies their reaction; he wrote that Pissarro "has a deplorable predilection for market-gardens. . . . But these errors of logic or vulgarities of taste do not alter his beautiful qualities of execution."

8

PLACE DU CARROUSEL, PARIS
1900
Oil on canvas, 54.9 x 65.4 cm.
Ailsa Mellon Bruce Collection

In its luminous palette and free brushwork, *Place du Carrousel, Paris* resembles *Orchard in Bloom, Louveciennes,* even though Pissarro painted the urban scene some twenty-eight years after he painted the landscape. In the intervening years Pissarro abandoned impressionism in favor of neo-impressionism, but after Seurat's death in 1891 he decided the latter was sterile, a blind alley. He wrote that it was "hard work to find again what I had lost and not to lose what I had been able to learn." Hence the return to his impressionist style.

The subject of *Place du Carrousel, Paris* likewise recalls the early years of impressionism; in the 1860s and early 1870s many artists, among them Monet, Renoir, and Morisot, painted cityscapes depicting the changing face of Paris. Pissarro, however, had not. It was not until he revived his impressionist vocabulary in the 1890s that he also turned to this early impressionist theme. The difficulties with his vision that forced Pissarro to work indoors account in part for his choice of this subject, but Pissarro's growing admiration for Monet's innovative series paintings, particularly the Rouen Cathedral group, was also a large factor. As Monet had done in Rouen, Pissarro in 1899 and 1900 comfortably established himself in upper-story rooms along the rue de Rivoli in Paris. He commanded a sweeping panorama extending from the Louvre to the Arc de Triomphe at the center of the place du Carrousel, the parterres of the Tuileries Gardens, and skyline of the left bank.

Place du Carrousel, Paris, painted in 1900, belongs to a series of twenty-eight paintings depicting views from his window and is one of only four works in the series focusing on the place du Carrousel. As Monet had done in his Rouen Cathedral paintings, Pissarro studied the scene before him under differing weather conditions and times of day. The artist exhibited *Place du Carrousel, Paris* and thirteen others from this series of familiar landmarks in 1901.

9

EDOUARD
Manet

FRENCH, 1832–1883

STILL LIFE WITH MELON
AND PEACHES
c. 1866
Oil on canvas, 69 x 92.2 cm.
Gift of Eugene and Agnes E. Meyer

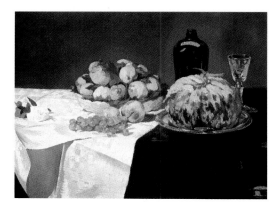

Still Life with Melon and Peaches is one of Manet's most ambitious still life paintings. Although it is part of a long tradition of seventeenth-century Spanish, Dutch and Flemish, and eighteenth-century French still lifes, this painting does not share the moralizing symbolism of many of those earlier works. Rather Manet has simply arranged, for our visual delectation, an array of fruits and one lone flower on a shimmering damask tablecloth. The elegance of this display is very much in keeping with Second Empire affluence and taste.

 Still Life with Melon and Peaches may be a pendant to another still life by Manet of similar dimensions, *The Salmon* (Shelburne Museum, Shelburne, Vermont). In their own time, Manet's still lifes achieved little popular and commercial success, probably for the very reasons we so admire them today: Manet's virtuoso touch and radical handling of the paint surface.

EDOUARD
Manet

FRENCH, 1832–1883

BALL AT THE OPERA
1873
Oil on canvas, 59 x 72.5 cm.
Gift of Mrs. Horace Havemeyer in memory of
her mother-in-law, Louisine W. Havemeyer

Every Saturday night during carnival season, masked balls were given at the opera house in rue Lepeletier in Paris. The gentlemen dressed in formal evening attire, while the women—assumed to be *demi-mondaines*—wore masks and costumes. Manet began this painting in the spring of 1873. Before he finished it the next autumn, however, the opera house had burned down. It was replaced, eventually, by Garnier's much more imposing and ornate structure. This picture has been interpreted as a nostalgic tribute to lively and slightly risqué evenings spent at the intimate old opera house.

Several of Manet's friends posed for this painting, but their identities in the picture are disputed. By general agreement, however, the man with the blond beard who looks out at us on the right is Manet himself. The absence of a single focus, the cropping of the Polichinelle on the left and of several anonymous figures on the right, and, most dramatically, the legs dangling from the balcony above all reinforce the informality of the occasion.

Manet submitted *Ball at the Opera* to the Salon of 1874, along with *Gare Saint-Lazare* (National Gallery of Art, Washington). The latter work was accepted, while this one was rejected. The first owner of this picture was the opera singer Jean-Baptiste Faure, who was one of the most active patrons of contemporary French painting.

⚜

11   BEFORE THE BALLET
c. 1888
Oil on canvas, 40 x 88.9 cm.
Widener Collection

EDGAR
Degas

FRENCH, 1834–1917

Inside a rehearsal hall, six costumed dancers ready themselves for performance; one pulls her stockings up, another adjusts her slippers, and in the background, the others limber up at the bar. The two foreground figures are seated in a rather confined area, perhaps the end of a passage into the room. The placement of the girl at the left side of

the bench and the position of her legs mark the abrupt expansion of pictorial space, and her foot points to the window, which separates the two halves of the composition.

As with many other paintings that remained in the artist's studio until his death, Degas modified the composition of *Before the Ballet* more than once after its inception. Extensive changes are most noticeable on the right side; still faintly visible are traces of two additional dancers standing just beyond the girl pulling up her stocking. Degas also shifted the positions of the nearer dancers' legs several times and transformed the

final layers of paint to present a softer, more pastel-like appearance.

From 1868 until the end of his career, Edgar Degas devoted hundreds of paintings, pastels, and drawings to the theme of dance. Degas' habitual, almost obsessive repetition of individual motifs as well as entire compositions was a means by which he sought to advance his art. Consequently, the subject of the ballet, an art of artificial gestures and poses perfected by repeated rehearsal, was especially appropriate for Degas. Like the dancers depicted in *Before the Ballet*, repetition was his means toward perfection.

12

PAUL
Cézanne

FRENCH, 1839–1906

STILL LIFE
c. 1900
Oil on linen, 45.8 x 54.9 cm.
Gift of the W. Averell Harriman Foundation
in memory of Marie N. Harriman

On stylistic grounds, this still life has been dated about 1900; soon after, it belonged to the artist's old friend Claude Monet, a noted gastronome in the artistic community. Unlike Cézanne's figure paintings and landscapes, objects in the still lifes, especially fruit, have such corporeal tangibility that his friend Gustave Geffroy wrote "they suggest the good smell of fruit." While the fruit—variously identified as a lemon with apples, oranges, or peaches—obviously could not have been reused, the milk pitcher, plate, and curtain appear in other works of various dates, suggesting that they were probably props in the artist's studio.

The still life seems a simple work, but the underlying composition is an arbitrary and complex scheme. Cézanne distorted the shapes of many objects; the rear edge of the table, for instance, is higher at the left than the right. Shifts in perspective complement those distortions: some objects have been depicted frontally, notably the fruit and the front of the table, while the table top, milk pitcher, and plate are shown from above. Only a pyramid of fruit maintains the white plate's precarious tilt. Further, details that seem inconsequential are in fact integral to the composition: the angle of the curtain in the upper right corner, for instance, echoes the angle of the lip and back edge of the pitcher and also counters the plunging thrust of the right edge of the table. Here Cézanne reveals his peculiar gift for ably combining numerous disparate perceptions to form a cohesive, convincing composition.

Cézanne once punned that he wanted to shock Paris with his apples, alluding not only to the Parisians' almost inevitable disapproval of his art but also to the myth of the Judgment of Paris and the reward of love that the shepherd Paris gained by selecting Venus, by inference associating the apple with beauty and sexual fulfillment. That joking statement may help explain a paradox in Cézanne's mature oeuvre: his still lifes, in spite of their pedestrian subject, are among his most sensuous later works.

ALFRED
Sisley

FRENCH, 1839–1899

BOULEVARD HÉLOÏSE, ARGENTEUIL
1872
Oil on canvas, 39.5 x 59.6 cm.
Ailsa Mellon Bruce Collection

Boulevard Héloïse, Argenteuil is the result of one of Sisley's visits to the village where Monet lived and was perhaps even painted in his company, because there is an almost identical view of the same fog-bound street by Monet. While Monet emphasized the broad, smooth sweep of the modern boulevard, Sisley concentrated on its rural aspects in his painting, giving prominence to the horse-drawn cart, ruts in the road, and irregularity in the houses. The boulevard was, in fact, one of Argenteuil's principal streets, abutting the Promenade, which Monet painted in 1872 (see Plate 16). The trees at the right are the shared border between the busy street and the parklike Promenade.

ALFRED
Sisley

FRENCH, 1839–1899

MEADOW
1875
Oil on linen, 54.9 x 73 cm.
Ailsa Mellon Bruce Collection

Pissarro once called Alfred Sisley the perfect impressionist painter. Unlike Monet, Renoir, and Pissarro, Sisley concentrated almost exclusively on landscape, and although the other founders of impressionism consciously altered their styles, Sisley remained consistently impressionist throughout his career. Unlike his fellow impressionists and in spite of that fidelity—or perhaps because of it—Sisley did not achieve commercial success or public acceptance until after his death.

His paintings, particularly those of the mid-1870s, describe the scenery of France with direct and lyric simplicity. Executed in 1875, *Meadow* epitomizes Sisley's impressionism. Here, gently rolling pastures spread out under a sky made bluer by the contrasting white puffs of cloud. Sisley's handling responded to the individual components of the landscape before him: a loose web of rapid, slender touches form the wildflowers and grasses in the foreground, while broad strokes of pigment shape the more distant meadows. Sisley created soft and subtle contrasts in shade and tonality although he used the full range of impressionist color. As he explained, "the charm of a picture is many-sided. The subject, the motif, must always be set down in a simple way, easily understood and grasped by the beholder. By the elimination of superfluous detail the spectator should be led along the road that the painter indicates to him, and from the first be made to notice what the artist himself has felt."

CLAUDE
Monet

FRENCH, 1840–1926

BAZILLE AND CAMILLE
1865
Oil on canvas, 93 x 68.9 cm.
Ailsa Mellon Bruce Collection

During the spring and summer of 1865, Monet lived in Chailly, near the forest of Fontainebleau. He moved there to work on the *Déjeuner sur l'herbe,* a picture of his elegantly dressed friends gathered for a picnic in the woods. The most ambitious undertaking of Monet's early career, the *Déjeuner* was inspired by Manet's canvas of the same title that had been the sensation of the Salon des Refusés in 1863. *Camille and Bazille* is an oil study, painted *en plein air,* for two figures in Monet's painting. The models were the artist Frédéric Bazille, whom Monet had met a few years earlier in Gleyre's studio in Paris, and Camille Doncieux, who lived with Monet and became his wife in 1870.

After executing a preliminary sketch for the entire *Déjeuner* composition (Pushkin Museum of Fine Arts, Moscow), Monet began painting the final canvas, which measured 15 x 20 feet. He intended to submit the work to the Salon of 1866, but did not finish it in time. He subsequently cut up the picture, preserving only two pieces. One of the fragments depicts Bazille and Camille in poses nearly identical to those in the National Gallery's sketch (Musée d'Orsay, Paris).

16

CLAUDE
Monet

FRENCH, 1840–1926

ARGENTEUIL
c. 1872
Oil on canvas, 50.4 x 65.2 cm.
Ailsa Mellon Bruce Collection

After the Franco-Prussian War, the artists now known as the impressionists began moving to suburban villages along the Seine, such as Argenteuil, a short distance from Paris. In this painting, Monet depicts the bucolic charm and quiet that drew people, especially the *haute bourgeoisie,* away from Paris. Among the principal attractions was sailing, a sport for which Argenteuil had become particularly famous and which was then in vogue among the wealthier newcomers. Only two sailboats are out, and just three women linger under the trees, while the factories beyond are idle. Afternoon light spills through trees lining the Promenade, a park along the Seine, belying the anxieties and difficulties facing a nation that had recently suffered the loss of a devastating war with Prussia.

17

CLAUDE
Monet

FRENCH, 1840–1926

THE ARTIST'S GARDEN
AT VÉTHEUIL
1880
Oil on canvas, 151.4 x 121 cm.
Ailsa Mellon Bruce Collection

Monet's most famous garden was the water garden he
created at Giverny, but it was not his only one. Throughout his adult life Monet gardened, first at Argenteuil
(seen in Renoir's *Madame Monet and Her Son,* Plate 21)
and then at Vétheuil, where his landlady allowed him to
cultivate land opposite the house leading to the Seine
embankment. The ascending steps and path and the
massed sunflowers that flank them mask a roadway that
separated the garden from the houses beyond. Painted
toward the end of Monet's Vétheuil period, one of the
most difficult phases of his career, *The Artist's Garden
at Vétheuil* nonetheless depicts a sunny haven remote
from incessant familial and financial anxieties.

18

BERTHE
Morisot

FRENCH, 1841–1895

THE ARTIST'S SISTER AT A WINDOW
1869
Oil on canvas, 54.8 x 46.3 cm.
Ailsa Mellon Bruce Collection

The story of this charming portrait is preserved in correspondence between Berthe Morisot and her mother in Paris, and her sister, Edma Pontillon, living in Lorient. Until Edma's marriage in 1869, she and Berthe had never been separated; longing to see her sister, Berthe was allowed to spend the summer with her. When Berthe returned home in early August, Mme Morisot wrote Edma, "I thought the two paintings she brought back very pretty; they do quite well in the studio and I will hang your sketch with pleasure, although Berthe forbids my putting it where people will see." Later that year, anticipating Edma's stay in Paris for the birth of her first child, Berthe wrote, "Manet recommended that I slightly retouch the portrait I made of you, so when you arrive I hope you will let me redraw the hands and make a few finishing touches to the bottom of your dress; that's all it wants. He told me that my Salon entry is assured and that I shouldn't torment myself, then he immediately added that of course I will be rejected." Manet probably intended the latter as a compliment; Salon juries in the 1860s, notorious for their bias against new tendencies in painting, had rejected many of Manet's own submissions. Both of Morisot's entries, *The Artist's Sister at a Window* and *The Mother and Sister of the Artist,* were accepted for the Salon of 1870, although Morisot later complained that the former was badly hung.

Close ties existed between the Morisot and Manet families from the late 1860s, and during the winter of 1868–1869 Berthe was able to watch the older artist at work when she posed for *The Balcony.* By the summer of 1869 Morisot had adapted those aspects of Manet's style, especially his summary execution and freer brushwork, which suited her temperament. In *The Artist's Sister at a Window* broad areas of paint like Manet's are charged with a refined nervous energy unique to Morisot.

Edma's abstracted toying with her fan is the kind of keenly observed gesture that animates Morisot's work and reveals the sisters' intimacy, but the painting could not properly be called a portrait. *The Artist's Sister at a Window* is an odd picture: Edma sits in a chair placed by the window but takes no interest in the balcony or the street beyond, as though the artist placed her there simply to take advantage of the fall of light on her white dress. Like Manet's depiction of Berthe in *The Balcony,* Berthe's portrayal of her sister here is more the expression of an interior mood than an external face.

19

BERTHE
Morisot

FRENCH, 1841–1895

THE HARBOR AT LORIENT
1869
Oil on fabric, 43.5 x 73 cm.
Ailsa Mellon Bruce Collection

The Harbor at Lorient, like *The Artist's Sister at a Window* (see Plate 18), was painted during Morisot's summer visit to her sister Edma in 1869, and Edma appears here, too, seated on a parapet overlooking the harbor. By this time Morisot was within Manet's circle, but aside from her choice of a modern subject,

this painting instead bears evidence of Corot's continuing influence on his former pupil. As with his *River Scene with Bridge* (see Plate 1), Morisot painted outdoors, and like Corot she laid in the broad shape of her composition before defining its features more crisply. Unlike Corot, however, Morisot considered this a finishing painting, not a sketch. When she returned to Paris at summer's end, Manet visited her studio and so admired *The Harbor at Lorient* that she presented it to her friend, mentor, and future brother-in-law.

⚜

20

AUGUSTE
Renoir

FRENCH, 1841–1919

PONT NEUF, PARIS
1872
Oil on linen, 75.3 x 93.7 cm.
Ailsa Mellon Bruce Collection

Renoir, in hope of attracting new patrons, organized a public auction in March 1875 at Hôtel Drouot in Paris and persuaded Claude Monet, Berthe Morisot, and Alfred Sisley to participate. "The others shared my enthusiasm for the plan," he later told Ambroise Vollard, adding that they had selected "choice canvases—at least *we* thought them choice," but that the result was abysmal: "After it was over, the expenses had not even been covered; we actually owed money to the auctioneers!" Of the four painters Renoir fared the worst, and most of the paintings he did sell went for less than one hundred francs. *Pont Neuf, Paris* was the exception; its price, three hundred francs, was the highest obtained for any of his paintings.

The genesis of *Pont Neuf, Paris,* unlike many works of art, is well documented. Renoir's younger brother Edmond, who related the story some years later, was a budding journalist in 1872. The pair were permitted to occupy an upper floor of a café overlooking the Pont Neuf, allowing Edmond to write while Auguste painted the view before them of the bridge, the statue of Henri IV, and the Ile de la Cité buildings. On occasion the artist sent his brother outside to engage people in brief conversations, stopping them long enough for Renoir to capture their appearance. A jaunty straw-hatted stroller carrying a cane pauses in the road near the center of the painting; he also appears again at the left, walking onto the bridge. That is Edmond. Renoir's economical strokes wittily characterize his brother and the cross section of the populace that happened to pass that day.

Although best known for his figures, it was Renoir's originality as a landscape painter that was instrumental in the formation of impressionism. Here, that originality is most apparent in the artist's use of light. Sunlight animates the entire scene, its midday intensity suppressing incidental detail; figures are defined with few broad strokes, while a web of spontaneous, thin touches articulates the architecture beyond. The sun also brightened the artist's palette. The pavement is yellow with light, and a complementary blue, rather than a black or gray, describes shadows along the parapet, while the deep blue of the sky, echoed by the Seine, casts its watery reflection on place du Vert Galant at the base of the statue.

Pont Neuf, Paris is a sparkling view across the oldest Parisian bridge toward the Ile de la Cité, the heart of modern Paris and site of its ancient origin. Renoir's crowds passing along the bustling thoroughfare betray no sign of either the devastation wrought by Prussian occupation of the city or the ensuing violent suppression of the Commune, events which had occurred only a year earlier. Rather, the painting not only affirms but even pays homage to the strength of the French people and vitality of the nation.

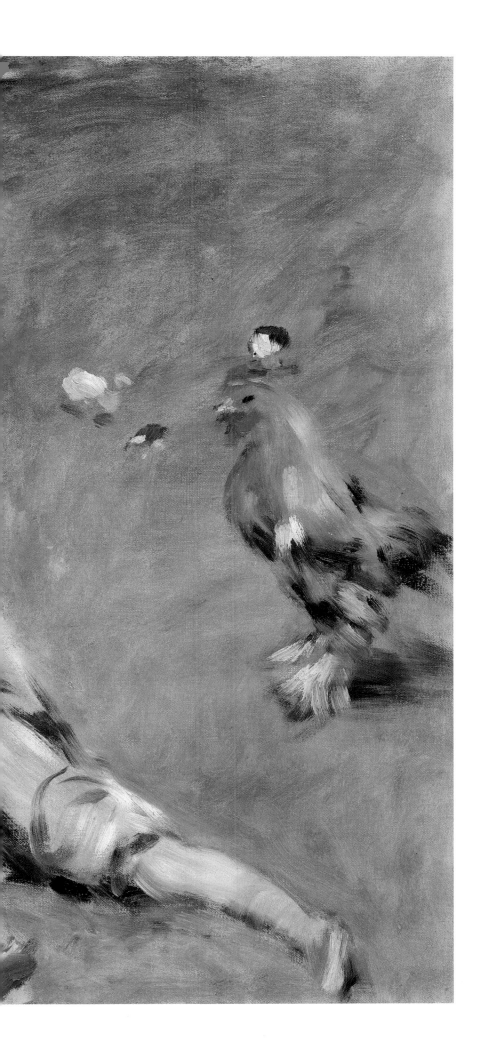

21

AUGUSTE *Renoir*

FRENCH, 1841–1919

MADAME MONET AND HER SON
1874
Oil on canvas, 50.4 x 68 cm.
Ailsa Mellon Bruce Collection

The origins of *Madame Monet and Her Son* are well known. As Monet later recalled:

> This delightful painting by Renoir, of which I am the happy owner today, portrays my first wife. It was done in our garden at Argenteuil. One day, Manet, enthralled by the color and light, undertook an outdoor painting of figures under the trees. During the sitting, Renoir arrived. He, too, was caught up in the spirit of the moment. He asked me for palette, brush, and canvas, and there he was, painting away alongside Manet. The latter was watching him out of the corner of his eye, and from time to time came over for a closer look at the canvas. Then he made a face, passed discretely near me, and whispered in my ear about Renoir: 'He has no talent, that boy! Since he's your friend, tell him to give up painting! . . .' Wasn't that amusing of Manet?

Manet then owned an early portrait by Renoir, and is known to have preferred it to Renoir's more recent works, but his comment was not necessarily serious. By 1874, Manet, too, was beginning to work in an impressionist manner. At any rate, Renoir's fluid handling, especially in the lush amplitude of Mme Monet's dress and the child's easy sprawl, and incisive delineation of such details as the black ribbon around her neck and the fan in her hand are compelling evidence of his mastery of all aspects of the technique that only recently had been labelled impressionism by a sarcastic critic.

22

MARY
Cassatt

AMERICAN, 1844–1926

CHILDREN PLAYING ON THE BEACH
1884
Oil on canvas, 97.4 x 74.2 cm.
Ailsa Mellon Bruce Collection

In 1884 Mary Cassatt accompanied her convalescent mother to Spain. *Children Playing on the Beach* is probably a product of that journey. Its charm captivated critics who first saw the painting in 1886 at the last of the impressionist group exhibitions. One writer praised its "naturalism and truth," while another commented: "Two chubby-cheeked babies dig chasms in the sand that a drop of water will fill, two babies with cheeks like jam, intent on their games, not heeding the roaring of the waves."

Although it appears uncomplicated, this depiction of two unknown little girls at play in the sand was in fact laboriously achieved. Cassatt extensively reworked the canvas, suggesting that although begun in Spain the painting was probably not completed until her return to Paris. While the most obvious changes in design appear in the figures of the children, especially in the placement and contours of their limbs, Cassatt modified almost every area of the composition, reducing the number of boats and altering their placement as well as removing several objects from the sandy expanse of beach. The uncluttered setting heightens the girls' isolation, enhancing Cassatt's depiction of the carefree innocence of children. Cassatt is best known for paintings of children's private moments, but, curiously, despite the praise *Children Playing on the Beach* received, and the attraction beach motifs held for such fellow painters of modern life as Boudin, Degas, Manet, Morisot, and Renoir, this is the only beach scene Cassatt painted.

Edgar Degas introduced Cassatt to the impressionist group in 1877 and she valued his artistic advice and opinions. While attending an exhibition in Cassatt's company, Degas scornfully denied that any woman could recognize quality in art; Cassatt painted *Girl Arranging Her Hair* (National Gallery of Art, Washington) to prove him wrong, and exhibited it, along with *Children Playing on the Beach*, at the 1886 impressionist show. Like *Girl Arranging Her Hair, Children Playing on the Beach* may once have belonged to Degas, and like the other painting could have demonstrated to Degas that women could indeed equal their male counterparts.

⚜

23

GUSTAVE
Caillebotte

FRENCH, 1848–1894

SKIFFS
1877
Oil on canvas, 88.9 x 116.2 cm.
Collection of Mr. and Mrs. Paul Mellon

Along with horse-racing and other English sports, boating became especially popular in France under the Second Empire. As rail travel made the suburbs outside Paris increasingly accessible, city dwellers—including the impressionists—retreated to the villages on the Seine for weekends and holidays. In this painting, Caillebotte depicted light-weight, flat-bottomed skiffs called *périssoires,* on a narrow, wooded stretch of the Yerres river near his family's country estate.

Caillebotte established his reputation in the second and third impressionist exhibitions in 1876 and 1877, with a series of ambitious Parisian interiors and street scenes in which he combined traditional realist technique with unconventional spatial constructions. *Skiffs* is one of a number of paintings of boaters and bathers Caillebotte executed in the following years and exhibited at the fourth impressionist show in 1879. In these works, he introduced the heightened palette and broken brushstrokes of his friends Monet, Renoir, and Sisley. He continued to experiment with perspectival effects. Here he cropped out almost the entire skiff on the right, and employed a point of view so low that the spectator is nearly at water's level, and the figures of the boaters are radically foreshortened.

24

PAUL
Gauguin

FRENCH, 1848–1903

BRETON GIRLS DANCING, PONT-AVEN
1888
Oil on canvas, 73 x 92.7 cm.
Collection of Mr. and Mrs. Paul Mellon

In mid-June 1888, Gauguin wrote his dealer, Vincent van Gogh's brother Theo, "I'm doing a *gavotte bretonne,* three little girls dancing in a hayfield. . . .The painting seems original to me and I'm quite pleased with the composition." The artist transliterated the sinuous movement of a peasant dance into the pattern of undulating curves in the girls' linked arms and their traditional white collars and intricately folded headdresses.

In the background is the village of Pont-Aven, a farming community with a thriving artists' colony. Paris and Parisian art seemed over-sophisticated and false to Gauguin, so he went to Brittany in July 1886. In 1888 he wrote, "I like Brittany, it is savage and primitive," but less than a year after he painted *Breton Girls Dancing, Pont-Aven,* Pont-Aven became too crowded for Gauguin. He moved first to Le Pouldu, more isolated and primitive, but, again dissatisfied, Gauguin eventually left France in search of an untainted tropical paradise in the Pacific.

PAUL
Gauguin

FRENCH, 1848–1903

THE BATHERS
1897
Oil on canvas, 60.4 x 93.4 cm.
Gift of Sam A. Lewisohn

Painted in 1897, *The Bathers* dates from Gauguin's second Polynesian period. After his first trip to Tahiti, from 1891 to 1893, he returned to Paris for two years, to arrange for exhibitions and—he hoped—sales of his works. In 1895, Gauguin returned to the South Seas, where he remained until his death in 1903, on a remote island in the Marquesas. During these last years of his life, Gauguin was often ill and destitute, but he continued to produce idyllic visions of his exotic paradise. Soon after executing this contemplative and essentially decorative painting, Gauguin began the most ambitious and philosophical project of his late career, *Where do we come from? What are we? Where are we going?* (Museum of Fine Arts, Boston).

In *The Bathers,* four women gather under blossoming trees beside a quiet stream of water. The canvas is thinly painted on rough burlap, in a rainbow of muted hues. Gauguin may have intended *The Bathers* as a tribute to Cézanne, who executed a number of compositions of similar subjects. This picture once belonged to Degas, who was an early patron of Gauguin.

VINCENT
van Gogh

DUTCH, 1853–1890

FLOWER BEDS IN HOLLAND
c. 1883
Oil on canvas mounted on wood, 48.9 x 66 cm.
Collection of Mr. and Mrs. Paul Mellon

Flower Beds in Holland, one of van Gogh's earliest surviving works, was probably painted at The Hague in the spring of 1883. The expressive use of color and rich surface texture for which his mature works are known are already evident here: the flower beds are described by thick, vertical strokes in contrast to the silhouetted, calligraphically flat tree branches. Moreover, in focusing on the vivid profusion of the growing flowers and the dark huddled homes of the peasants who worked in the fields depicted, van Gogh reflects an early interest in subjects that he would continue to treat throughout his career.

27

VINCENT
van Gogh

DUTCH, 1853–1890

FARMHOUSE IN PROVENCE, ARLES
1888
Oil on canvas, 46.1 x 60.9 cm.
Ailsa Mellon Bruce Collection

The winter of 1887–1888 was particularly harsh in Paris, to the detriment of van Gogh's already precarious health. In February he left for Arles, a small town in the south of France. As well as hoping that the warmer climate would improve his generally debilitated condition, Vincent later enumerated other motives for his departure in a letter to his brother Theo:

> I came to the South and threw myself into my work for a thousand reasons. Wishing to see a different light, thinking that looking at nature under a bright sky might give us a better idea of the Japanese way of feeling and drawing. Wishing also to see this stronger sun . . ., because one feels that the colors of the prism are veiled in the mist of the North.

The oriental-inspired rhythmic swirls and flourishes of van Gogh's brush charge this placid farmyard with nervous energy. Wildflowers made of thick, pure red dots atop spiky green foliage enliven the foreground. The contrast between the bulky, irregular haystacks and the spare, angular house and gateposts in *Farmhouse in Provence, Arles* must have appealed to the artist; this is one of several paintings and drawings depicting the same house, gate, and haystacks.

In the second week of June 1888, van Gogh wrote his sister:

> The sun in these parts, *that* is something different. . . . I feel it is excellent for me to work in the open air during the hottest part of the day. It is airy, clean heat. Essentially the color is exquisite here. When the green leaves are fresh, it is a rich green, the like of which we seldom see in the North. When it gets scorched and dusty, it does not lose its beauty, for then the landscape gets tones of gold of various tints, green-gold, yellow-gold, pink-gold, and in the same way bronze, copper, in short starting from citron yellow all the way to a dull, dark yellow color like a heap of threshed corn, for instance. And this combined with the blue—from the deepest royal blue of the water to the blue of the forget-me-nots, cobalt, particularly clear, bright blue—green-blue and blue-violet. Of course, this calls up orange—a sunburned face gives the impression of orange. Furthermore, on account of the many yellow hues, violet gets a quick emphasis; a cane fence or a gray thatched roof or a dug-up field makes a much more violet impression than at home.

When van Gogh wrote this description, he was concurrently working on the small group of farm scenes which includes *Farmhouse in Provence, Arles*. Although he did not refer directly to any particular painting, van Gogh described their content in detail; all the colors he catalogued, for instance, appear in this painting. In addition, his words invest the farm paintings with deeper significance. Under the southern sun the colors of nature are brilliantly transformed, and, as he assured his sister, the sun was excellent for him, an allusion to his then-improving health. Van Gogh's farm paintings do not merely depict the physical character of the Provençal countryside, they represent the goodness and beauty of the sun.

GEORGES
Seurat

FRENCH, 1859–1891

STUDY FOR "LA GRANDE JATTE"
1884/1885
Oil on wood, 15.9 x 25 cm.
Ailsa Mellon Bruce Collection

The most-discussed painting at the eighth and last of the impressionist group exhibitions in 1886 was a massive painting by Georges Seurat, *Un Dimanche à la Grande Jatte*, which propelled the artist to the forefront of the avant-garde. The small painting exhibited here is one of the many oil sketches and drawings Seurat executed in preparation for the larger work. The light brown wooden panel visible through the paint is actually the top of a cigar box. Short dashes of pigment—which in the finished work were transformed into the now famous "pointillist" dots—to describe bourgeois and working-class Sunday visitors to a park on an island in the Seine a short distance from Paris.

GEORGES
Seurat

FRENCH, 1859–1891

SEASCAPE AT PORT-EN-BESSIN, NORMANDY
1888
Oil on linen, 65.1 x 80.9 cm.
Gift of the W. Averell Harriman Foundation
in memory of Marie N. Harriman

Georges Seurat developed neo-impressionism to systematize—and thereby more accurately depict scientifically observed facts of nature—the spontaneous irregularity of impressionist techniques. That is, he thought that the use of small dots of pure pigment and application of theories of optical mixture and simultaneous contrast would allow greater fidelity to nature than previously had been possible by enabling him to render daylight with more precision. Early in 1888 Seurat completed two large studio works, *La Parade* and *Les Poseuses,* in which he applied newly formulated aesthetic principles of composition to complement his earlier theories of paint application. As the artist later explained: "Art is Harmony. Harmony is the analogy of contrary and of similar elements of *tone,* of *color,* and of *line,* considered according to their dominants and under the influence of light, in gay, calm, or sad combinations. . . . Sadness of *tone* is given by the dominance of dark; of *color,* by the dominance of cold colors; and of *line,* by downward direction."

Perhaps as much to assure himself that this theory was indeed applicable to landscape painting as to refresh his vision after an intensive winter campaign in his studio, the artist spent the summer, as he had often done before, on the northern coast of France, in the fishing village of Port-en-Bessin. When he returned to Paris he took back only six unfinished works, among them this seascape. *Seascape at Port-en-Bessin, Normandy* is so accurately observed and recorded that Seurat must have climbed the headlands west of town to the falaise de Huppain. Planting his easel there, he faced west toward the Cotentin peninsula to depict the sloping cliffs and the sea lighted by the afterglow of sunset.

In addition to their striking fidelity to the terrain, Seurat's Port-en-Bessin paintings equally demonstrate the remarkable effectiveness of the artist's complex aesthetic principles. Seurat apparently intended that this painting express sadness. He carefully selected his pictorial means to create the prescribed equivalencies of tone, color, and line to correspond to the landscape depicted: the painting is relatively dark, cool blues and greens dominate, and the undulating profile of the cliffs falls diagonally toward the sea. The sun has fallen, and dark clouds press down over a single ship in the distance. Absolutely devoid of movement, the painting is melancholy and elegaic. Seurat had turned away from the naturalist impulse that earlier inspired him to invent neo-impressionism and toward a scientifically-based language of abstract signs that he used like a poet.

30

PIERRE
Bonnard

FRENCH, 1867–1947

BOUQUET OF FLOWERS
c. 1926
Oil on canvas, 70.3 x 47.4 cm.
Ailsa Mellon Bruce Collection

This still life, lush pink flowers seen with a red and white plaid tablecloth, differs markedly from Bonnard's earlier works. His brushwork here is freer, and his use of color ebullient in comparison. Bonnard was unaffected by cubism; rather, he continued to develop the decorative qualities apparent even in works from the beginning of his career.

31

EDOUARD
Vuillard

FRENCH, 1868–1940

CHILD WEARING A RED SCARF
c. 1891
Oil on cardboard mounted on wood, 29.2 x 17.5 cm.
Ailsa Mellon Bruce Collection

With his close friend Bonnard, Vuillard was part of the nabi group, a loosely affiliated group of younger artists inspired by the example of Gauguin's Breton paintings (see Plate 24). Each different color area in *Child Wearing a Red Scarf* is treated as an outlined block of pigment distinct from the others, with no shadows for modeling. Roundness is suggested only by the colors and shapes themselves, as in the curving orange scarf around the girl's shoulders. Another of the nabis, Maurice Denis, wrote in 1890: "One must remember that a painting is primarily a flat surface covered with colors organized in a certain order; its identity as a focus for discussion, a nude woman or an anecdote, is firmly subordinate." One reason for the painting's appeal is that, while working within those constraints, Vuillard, by adopting a low point of view, was able, like Cassatt (see Plate 22), to evoke the child's innocent view of the world.

32

EDOUARD
Vuillard

FRENCH, 1868–1940

THE CONVERSATION
1891
Oil on canvas, 23.8 x 33.4 cm.
Ailsa Mellon Bruce Collection

For most of his career, Vuillard lived with his mother, a widowed seamstress, in successive Paris apartments that also served as his mother's workshop. Many of his intimist works depict that shared, small world. Mme Vuillard is the woman standing at the near side of the table, and one of her shop assistants or perhaps the artist's sister faces her in this confined space. *The Conversation* seems a deceptive title for this painting; silence reigns in the narrow room.